*Kensington
in old photographs*

Tower House in Melbury Road

Kensington
in old photographs

compiled by
BARBARA DENNY
from the collection in Kensington Central Library

LONDON AS IT WAS

CBL Publishing

First published 1974 by
CBL Publishing Development Ltd
16 Pembridge Road   London W11

Printed in the UK by Kingprint Ltd
Orchard Road, Richmond, Surrey

0 904500 01 2

Contents

Introduction

	photograph nos
Kensington High Street	1-35
Kensington Church Street & Campden Hill	36-51
Northern Kensington	52-64
Notting Hill & Holland Park	65-80
Earl's Court	81-89
Southern Kensington	90-105
Knightsbridge	106-111
Kensington life	112-143

The compiler would like to acknowledge the help and encouragement given by the staff of the Royal Borough of Kensington & Chelsea Libraries, and in particular by Mr. Brian Curle, over the preparation of this book.

Kensington Old Toll Gate

Introduction

The traveller who entered Kensington 300 years ago, and the visitor of today, as like as not came in by the same roads, changed though now they may be.

From the west to the east, whether by the old turnpikes, or the M4 or the M40, from the north to the south, forced to digress by the geographical circumstance of hilly ground, or the boundaries of the royal parklands of Kensington Palace, the modern traveller takes much the same way as his predecessors, by Counters Creek, or past the former farmlands of Portobello.

Further south, the few bridges and ferries over a then wider Thames dictated the lines of the roads that still run down to the river, choked now with the overweight traffic of modern London.

A century and a half ago, the grey mass of bricks and mortar which makes up Kensington, with its periodic contradictions of commerce and culture, elegance and depressing mediocrity, sometimes veering into squalor, was a collection of rural communities, set up around the big houses of the rich, aristocratic or merchant, already moving out from a noisy and crowded city centre.

In less than fifty years during the nineteenth century, villages disappeared, swallowed up by the infectious rash of largely speculative building. The railways pierced south, north, east and west. Orchards were felled, pastures ploughed up, terraces of villas lined the few original lanes, and new roads crossed and criss-crossed each other in a maze of development.

In the years between 1821 and 1901 the population of Kensington alone increased from 14,428 to 176,628.

Even so, those days of rural Kensington are only just fading from living memory. There are still near centenarians who can recall cows being milked near the Holland Arms in Kensington High Street, and stables on what is now a car park at the corner of Earls Court Road.

More recent memories are of repeated urban developments, of cottages knocked down to build a school, which in its turn was demolished to build a supermarket; of a Barker's store that stood before the present Barker's, and a Notting Hill Gate that was Victorian, not neo-concrete.

The pictures in this book will remind those who can remember of the old Kensington which is already fading from memory, and show those who are too young to have seen it for themselves, the past from which the present has evolved.

It is not always a romantic past. Much of what has gone was as ugly, or even uglier, than that which has replaced it. Many of the buildings which surrendered to the destruction of the bulldozers were lovely only insofar as they were loved by those who lived or worked in them. Others had charm or elegance in their own right and can be mourned for this.

Some left the ghosts of their outlines behind them, so that in a roof-line here, the turn of a road there, you can still catch a glimpse of the past, despite the facade of modernity, neon signs, plastic, paint and plaster.

When practically all has gone and the modern road itself is twice as wide (as is the case with Kensington High Street and Notting Hill Gate) it is difficult to believe that the very ground on which you are standing is the same as that where horses' hooves clattered over cobbles, carts rumbled and cattle were driven to market.

Even when Mr. Barker, Mr. Derry and Mr. Toms opened their first drapers' shops in the 1870s opposite the newly built St. Mary Abbots church and Mr. Jubal Webb's cheese shop, the High Street, being lined with lower buildings than today, was a lighter, brighter, though narrower road.

Along the High Street towards Hammersmith, the shops on the northern side were set up on a raised pavement which protected pedestrians from the dirt thrown up by passing horse-buses and carriages. An old lady of over ninety can recall her habit in childhood of giving the crossing sweeper a penny. Here and there, more than 100 years ago, could be seen at least a few names which are still flourishing today, such as the estate agents, Chestertons, (founded by the grandfather of GK) which still stands on its original site, although in a new building. Gone, though, is the Kensington Wheeling Depot, which was renowned for the adventurous bicycle as well as hand-carts and perambulators.

Towards the east and the park (where the old inn sign of the Civet Cat still hangs above the modern frontage of a bank) the Royal Palace Hotel, which seemed so huge to the Edwardians who danced in its ballroom, was felled, and its shade dwarfed by the Royal Garden Hotel, which now completely dominates this end of the street and obscures the view of the park beyond, so as to give the illusion of a cul-de-sac.

John Barker's original plate-glass promenade retired backwards to be replaced by many storeys of columned stone, and Derrys, famous for its hats before its roof garden, and with a beautiful curved glass window near the station, succumbed first to 1930s architecture and then to Biba in the 1970s.

Families sat down to nursery tea in Leonards Terrace, where the Odeon now hangs on precariously in the face of threatened development, and civil servants who work at

Charles House further west must scarcely believe that their gaunt offices occupy the site of the last gracious crescent which Kensington could boast on its boundary.

St. Mary Abbots Terrace has kept its name and lost its character. Its identity is now hidden behind high brick walls, and the houses have turned their backs on the High Street and taken with them the name plaques of doctors and dentists and veterinary surgeons, who once made up this 'profession row', neatly bordered with privet-hedges and lilacs.

The high walls of Holland House parklands used to shut out the view of prying eyes from Melbury Road to Phillimore Terrace, where the Commonwealth Institute now presents an open prospect of duckpond and flagpoles.

Higher up to the north, Lady Mary Coke, the 18th century albino beauty known as 'the white cat', and as a famous eccentric and diarist, who lived in Kensington's last surviving country home, Aubrey House on Campden Hill, used to sit on a hillock in her garden and watch the passing traffic on the road to Acton. If, in the spirit, she sits there still, she must be terrified by the nightmare growth around of towering buildings, far higher than her own elms. Even her facile pen might have been at a loss to describe such change, as one can imagine her trying to convey in one of her prolific letters — not only the passing of the old toll gate village of Notting Hill, but the Victorian gas-lit splendour of 'the Gate' in the 1890s, when the Coronet Theatre was in its glory, up to the radical changes of the 1950s when two thirds of the old town was swept away in a few months.

The Coronet remains, as 'the Gaumont', to act as a marker when the shadow of the past is superimposed on the present. Even then, it is hard to appreciate that this really is the same old street, where drapers' shops were selling lace at twopence three-farthings a yard, oil shops sold candles and nails from stacks of drawers instead of in plastic packets, grocers' stores smelled of cheese, coffee and brown suger, and 'tea shops' were neither trattoria nor pancake houses. (In fact the self-same road dates back to Roman times.)

Strangely enough, the further south you go, the less marked is the change. Brompton Road is still solidly Victorian, despite an effort to spread the modern trendiness of Chelsea. This is no doubt in part to do with Harrods, that fortress of a department store, which stands invincibly St. Pancras Gothic, against the invading forces of the Kings Road gear merchants. It is solidly supported on the west flank by the Museums, as Victorian as Kensington should be, (although one was opened in the Edwardian era).

Cromwell Road is succumbing to the hotel boom, close to the air terminal and beneath the jets which rip the air apart above it, bringing package tourists for one or two nights of doubtful repose in a luxury 'cell'. But between the concrete towers, some old grey houses hold out from the days when the road sweeper could still broom down the centre of the street at high noon without committing suicide!

Of nineteenth century Kensington, Fulham Road is the least touched by modern hands. Here and there someone built a cinema or put a new front on an old shop, but Fulham Road, hospitals and all (it has three) is still homely and 'family' in character, just like Gloucester Road and Ladbroke Grove (despite the latter being spanned by a new urban motorway).

Kensington Church Street suffers from the 'boutiques infection' at its lower end, but expensive antique shops hold on higher up, although the barracks in between, with its red-tiled 'public lavatory' walls which once housed the Royal Military Police, is now a hostel for students ('Oh, what a fall was there, my countrymen!'). But the past here is only a photographic negative away, easily replaced upon the present.

In fact, the past is never easily wiped away. Like a smear on glass, it may return even after the cloth has apparently wiped it clean. The fields go, but the trees live on in back gardens long years after those who planted them are dead and forgotten. A road still follows the same line because some medieval carter chose that way to ease the toil of his horse.

This book tries to lengthen the memory of this generation some years beyond the normal span, and to bring back some of the life that peopled the sticks and stones that are no more and those areas that remain.

In *The Napoleon of Notting Hill,* GK Chesterton's hero, Adam Wayne, was only speaking of his own town, but it could have been of anywhere that he said: 'It is a rise or high ground of the common earth on which men have built houses to live in, in which they are born, fall in love, pray, marry and die. These little gardens where we told our loves. These streets where we brought out our dead. Why should they be commonplace? There has never been anything in the world absolutely like them. There will never be anything quite like it to the crack of doom. And God loved it, as He must surely love anything which is itself and unreplaceable.'

Kensington High Street

1. This terrace of old shops, opposite the corner of Church Street, was demolished in the 1860s for a road-widening plan. The site is now occupied by Barker's department store.

2 (overleaf).   The Royal Palace Hotel, now demolished and replaced by the Royal
Garden Hotel, stands in a narrow of Kensington Road where cabs waited for fares
by the railings of Kensington Gardens.

3.   The new Royal Garden Hotel, built in Kensington High Street in 1970.

4. The eastern end of Kensington High Street, with the Royal Palace Hotel on the left.

5. 'Three well-appointed residences to be let', says the notice on Old Court Mansions above the (then new) Barker's building on the northern side of Kensington High Street at the turn of the century.

6. Looking east along the High Street, opposite the present site of the Royal Garden Hotel. Slater's shop later moved to premises on the other side of the road.

7. The 'Chocolate stick' memorial of Queen Victoria's Golden Jubilee stood at the junction of the High Street and Kensington Church Street, until it was moved to Warwick Gardens when the road was widened.

8. The eastern end of the High Street in 1893 before the Royal Palace Hotel was built. The terrace on the right now houses the Kensington antique market.

9. The post office in Young Street in the early 1900s.

10. Kensington Court, running south from the High Street.

11. The Kings Arms, in the High Street at the corner of Palace Avenue and demolished in 1892, was frequented by Joseph Addison and Thackeray, both of whom lived nearby. The latter used it as the setting for the climax of *Esmond*. This picture dates from Queen Victoria's Golden Jubilee celebrations in 1887.

12. Jubal Webb, cheesemonger, had his business in Kensington High Street, in premises which were later Mr. John Barker's first shop. When the Metropolitan Board decided to widen the road in the 1860s, Webb moved to the temporary premises shown here, next to old St. Mary Abbots Church, which was about to be demolished, later returning to a new shop at no. 34 on the south side of the street.

13 *(left)*. Originally built in 1852 as the Vestry Hall and re-opened in 1859 as the former Kensington Library, this building is still used as an annexe for council offices from the Town Hall next door. In this Edwardian photograph the vehicle in the road is a barrel-organ and behind are readers scanning the daily newspapers which were pasted onto a board along the wall.

14. Kensington Town Hall is seen in comparatively new Victorian splendour, in a section of the High Street not markedly different from today, apart from the traffic and the fashion boutiques.

15. The old Crown public house on the corner of Kensington Church Street is today a shoe shop.

16 *(above, right)*. Derry and Toms store on the south side of the High Street, with treetops visible on the famous roof garden. This modern photograph was taken shortly before Biba's moved into the building.

17 *(right)*. Ponting's store next to Derry & Toms was opened by the Ponting brothers who came to London from Gloucester in 1873. Since 1972 the building has been empty, and it is scheduled for demolition. Built on the site of Scarsdale House, it was adjacent to the site of a farm once owned by William Cobbett and the starting point for his 'Rural Rides'.

18 *(left)*. Kensington High Street station arcade.

19. A narrower but much brighter Kensington High Street than today, looking eastwards through the traffic to Mr. Barker's new store in the far distance.

20. The lodge gates at the entrance to Holland Park were demolished after the second world war, but the central ornamental gates, moved back from the roadway, remain well preserved today.

21. Holland House as it appeared in 1886. Most of this stately mansion, built in Elizabethan times for Sir Walter Cope (though the wings were added later), was destroyed in an air raid in the second world war. The cloisters remain and the house and grounds are now Holland Park, under GLC administration.

22. There were no shops on the north side of the High Street between Holland Park gates and Phillimore Terrace until the mid-1920s. These Victorian houses were in mainly professional occupation.

23. Outside the Town Hall on August 9 1914, the 13th (Princess Louis' Kensington) Battalion, the London Regiment hands its colours to the Mayor for safe keeping until their return from active service.

24 & 25. Leonard Place, the terrace of houses which stood on the present site of the Odeon cinema at the corner of Earls Court Road, were taken down in the late 1920s.

26. St. Mary Abbots Place, leading off the High Street towards its western end, in the early 1900s.

27. The Holland Arms, built 1866, as its facade proclaims in decorative brickwork, was demolished a century later, and a new pub built on its site in St. Mary Abbots Terrace.

28. Until the 1930s, St. Mary Abbots Terrace, which now ends at Addison Road, stretched from Melbury Road to Russell Road along the north side of Kensington High Street.

29. St. Mary Abbots Terrace from the corner of Addison Road, showing one of the houses with its own flagpole.

30. The corner of St. Mary Abbots Terrace and Addison Road looking west, and on the right the premises of Leslie March, estate agent, which were demolished in 1973.

31. This gracious sweep of Victorian houses, Kensington Crescent, was demolished before the second world war; it stood at the extreme west end of the High Street, and was replaced by the government offices of Charles House (no. 32, facing).

33. The 'Chocolate stick' memorial to Queen Victoria, standing today in Warwick Gardens, close to the Hammersmith border.

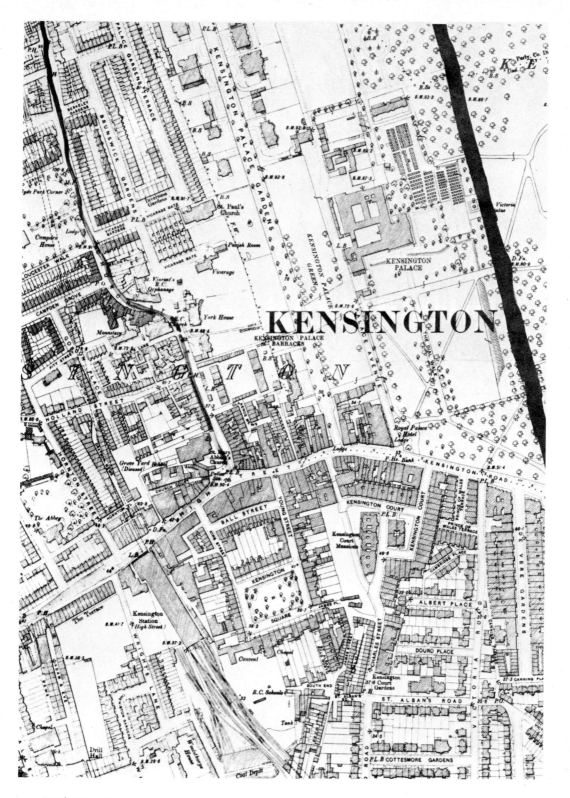

34. Kensington 1862–65.

35. Kensington 1894–96.

Kensington Church Street and Campden Hill

36. The Campden Hill water tower — G K Chesterton's 'great grey tower that strikes the stars on Campden Hill' — which was part of the Metropolitan Water Board's Grand Junction reservoir, and was dismantled in 1970, when the site was developed into a complex of flats.

37.   This terrace of houses from no. 1–5 Kensington Church Street, next to St. Mary Abbots Church, is now occupied by shops and boutiques. Here, before the first world war, in a photograph taken from the corner of Old Court Place, it included the premises of builders Simpson & Annett, and the House Boys Brigade.

38. St. Mary Abbots Church, demolished in 1869 because of its unsafe condition. The present church was consecrated in 1872.

39. Kensington Church Street at its southern end, before the building of the Gas, Light & Coke Company (latterly the North Thames Gas Board) offices on the left, at the corner of York House Place.

40 *(overleaf)*. Going, going, gone! These old houses at the northern end of Kensington Church Street were demolished in 1876 to make way for a new Board (later LCC) school. This part of Church Street was then known as Silver Street, and the school was demolished in its turn in the 1950s as part of the re-construction of Notting Hill Gate. The site now carries offices, shops and a supermarket . . .

41. . . . as you can see!

42. This veteran car in Vicarage Gate was probably the latest model when the photograph was taken early this century. In the background is the spire of St. Paul's Church, damaged by fire during the second world war, and later demolished.

43. The orphanage of St. Vincent de Paul on the corner of Kensington Church Street and Vicarage Gate was established in a former convent in the 1850s. It was replaced some 80 years later by a block of flats, Winchester Court, described at the time as 'decidedly the most meritorious building to appear in the area for a long time'. The railings just visible on the left surrounded the former Carmelite church, destroyed during the second world war and later re-built.

44. Riding in Percy Villas, now Sheffield Terrace, on Campden Hill. Most of the southern side of the street is now taken up by a block of flats.

45. Campden Street, long before it was transformed into the bijou homes of today. This and its surrounding area was built in the 1820s, and within fifty years had deteriorated into some of the worst slums in London.

46.   Campden Street looking east towards Church Street. The transformation since the second world war of cottages originally built for artisans into chic middle-class dwellings is one of the phenomena of west London in general and Kensington in particular.

47.   Peel Street, nearby, was built at much the same time, and by 1856 nearly all the houses were in multiple occupation. 'Pigs were kept there in a filthy condition', and there were 'foul and offensive privies', according to reports by contemporary authorities. The houses were let at rack rents of £12 per year. Part of the east end of Peel Street was demolished between 1865–75, and Campden House built as labourers' dwellings.

48. The offices of the *Kensington News* at 118 Church Street decorated for Queen Victoria's Diamond Jubilee in 1897. The paper, now merged with the *Kensington Post,* was founded in 1869 at this same address, then known as 4 Bedford Terrace. In this picture the staff are standing outside a window proudly boasting 'steam printing', and next door on the right is the Kensington Tea Market, later Madoc Jones grocers, and then Ellis Clibbon until closure in 1973.

49. Demolition of Edge Street and the corner of Kensington Church Street in the 1950s.

50. Hillgate Place, built as Dartmoor Street in the 1850s, within 20 years shared the reputation of its neighbour Johnson Street, now Hillgate Street, as a 'dingy ill-favoured slum'. In 1900 the vicar of St. George's Campden Hill made an appeal for the relief of the poverty of the inhabitants of the area, the conditions of whom, he said, 'were worse than the East End'.

51. Kensington Palace. 'Kingly Kensington', wrote Dean Swift, but Royal Kensington owes it regality as much to queens as to kings, although it was a king, William of Orange, who first set the royal seal upon a quiet countryside by selecting the Earl of Nottingham's compact home as the nucleus of his Kensington Palace; and for the next 150 years its warm red brick yet stately architecture was the bedrock of royal domesticity. Queen Anne, with her constant childbirths and her asthmatic husband Prince George, lived here, and the Hanoverian George the First found the palace agreeably like his native home. His son shared his liking, but George the Third deserted the palace, and it was not until 1819 that his son, Edward, Duke of Kent, returned to live there just one month before his wife bore the Princess Victoria. It was in the palace that Victoria learned of her accession to the throne, and it was by her later wish that her son, Edward the Seventh, created Kensington a Royal Borough, by charter.

Northern Kensington

52. Sound tomatoes at 4d a half-pound on W. Edwards' stall in Portobello Road in the 1920s.

53. Ladbroke Grove near the junction with Blenheim Crescent — little changed in the last 70 years.

54. Ladbroke Grove at the southern end, by the junction with Ladbroke Road.

55. Ladbroke Grove looking south from the corner of Cambridge Gardens, where today the railway bridge is dwarfed by the new viaduct carrying the M40 motorway.

56. Portobello Road near the corner of Cornwall Road

57. Portobello Road. 'The brass bottle' advertised on the side of the bus opened at the Vaudeville Theatre on October 16 1909, and thus dates this photograph of the Warwick Castle public house.

58. Portobello Road near the junction with Blenheim Crescent.

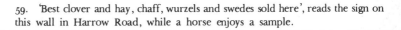

59. 'Best clover and hay, chaff, wurzels and swedes sold here', reads the sign on this wall in Harrow Road, while a horse enjoys a sample.

60. 'Eggs 8d a dozen, pure new country milk straight from the farm', sold by
Thomas's Dairy in All Saints Road in the 1900s.

61. Archer Street is now an extension of Westbourne Grove, and much of its
facade is relatively unchanged near the corner of Portobello Road.

62. Pembridge Road stretches north from Notting Hill Gate, and the facade shown here is little changed today.

63. Demolition of Blechynden Street, north Kensington, in advance of the construction of the M40 motorway in the early 1970s.

64. Kensal Green Cemetery, formed in 1832 by a joint stock company, is a splendid example of Victorian mausoleum construction in the monumental mode. Its seventy acres contain the graves of many celebrated people, not least the Duke of Sussex, son of George IV, who had declared he would prefer it to entombment at Windsor.

Notting Hill & Holland Park

65. The Coach & Horses at Notting Hill Gate.

66. Demolition prior to the reconstruction of Notting Hill Gate in the 1950s.

67. Notting Hill Underground station just before its redevelopment in the 1950s.

68. Looking west along Notting Hill Gate from the corner of Kensington Church Street, at a time when Finch's was selling pure brandy at 3s 6d a bottle. Moore's on the right are still famous for their teas.

69. The Coronet theatre in the early years of this century — it opened in 1898 with *The geisha*. Children from the surrounding neighbourhood were often recruited to take part in lavish spectaculars, in one case moving about under a giant sheet of green canvas to simulate waves at sea. The Coronet is now the Gaumont cinema.

70. The site of the present day Campden Hill Towers opposite the old Coronet, and looking westward.

71. The Towers today.

72. The Underground station today.

73. Parr's bank on the corner of Pembridge Gardens, which merged with the Westminster Bank after the first world war. The site is now occupied by a men's outfitters.

74. Notting Hill Gate between Kensington Church Street and Palace Gardens Terrace before the re-development of the 1950s.

75. Aubrey House, Campden Hill, as it is today. Formerly known as 'The Villa at Notting Hill', it was the home of the eighteenth century diarist Lady Mary Coke.

76. The old Mitre pub in Holland Park Avenue advertised 'Good accommodation for cyclists' when they were still the kings of the road at the turn of the century.

77. The old Central Line Underground station in Notting Hill Gate, between
Pembridge Road and Pembridge Gardens, opposite the Metropolitan station.

78. This street is called Holland Park, and an entrance to the park itself is just out
of sight on the left. The small trees there are now full grown.

79. Looking eastwards from the top of Holland Park Avenue into the beginning of Notting Hill Gate. Ladbroke Terrace is on the left.

80. Further down Holland Park Avenue, on the eastern
corner of Norland Square.

Earl's Court

81. The Manor Court House in Earl's Court Road, next to the present site of the Underground station.

82. Harness manufacturers and saddlery works in the terrace which still remains more than 60 years later at the western end of Pembroke Road.

83. Pembroke Road, Earl's Court, barely recognisable as the busy one-way traffic route it is today.

84. The northern end of Earl's Court Road, nos. 14 to 22, in 1910. Groom's, the fishmongers, remained until the terrace was emptied for re-development as the Odeon cinema site. Century Motors, far left, later became the parcels depot of Kensington Post Office.

85. Earl's Court Road opposite the present Underground station. Modern versions of the banks in this terrace are still there.

86 (overleaf). Earl's Court Farm in 1860–70. This photograph shows the farmer, Samuel Alloway, seated in the centre. Ensconsed in the cart nursing the dog is the foreman, Mr. Goddard. The farm stood on land now occupied by Earl's Court station, but in those days the old village of Earl's Court consisted of a few houses and cottages on the east side of the lane, with the farm and manor house on the west side. All around lay open farmland and market gardens. Development was rapid from the 1860s, and within 30 years the area was built up virtually to the density of today.

87. The Kensington Arms on the corner of Pembroke Road and Warwick Road.

88. The 300-foot Great Wheel of the Earl's Court Exhibition towers over houses in Philbeach Gardens.

89. Bramham Gardens, with a sign reading 'Organs and street cries prohibited'.

Southern Kensington

90. The horse, anticipating perhaps his impending redundancy, casts an anxious look at his supplanter, in the form of the Great Northern Piccadilly & Brompton Railway Station at South Kensington.

91. Old Brompton Road, looking eastward towards South Kensington station.

92 & 93. Hansom cabs and a horse-drawn bus are the only traffic to endanger
strolling pedestrians in Redcliffe Gardens.

94. The Gloucester public house on the corner of Gloucester Road and Victoria Grove looking towards Palace Gate at the turn of the century.

95. Gloucester Road looking up Palace Gate towards Kensington Gardens.

96. A streetsweeper and a milkman with his pony cart monopolise Edwardian
Gloucester Road.

97. Bailey's Hotel in Gloucester Road, just south of the Underground station. The bath chair, towed by an attendant, was a familiar sight in the streets of Edwardian London.

98. Old Brompton Road in the 1970s.

99. Gloucester Road between Queens Gate Terrace and Elvaston Place, with one side of the road still unbuilt.

100. Rival forms of transport in Cromwell Place, South Kensington in 1906. The horse-drawn bus belongs to the London General Omnibus Company and confronts two 'pirate' motor buses.

101. Horse-drawn traffic and a violinist in Harrington Road, South Kensington.

102. Cromwell Road, with two motor cars visible in the distance.

103. Stocken & Co., on the right, proudly announce that they are 'Carriage and motor builders to the King and the Prince of Wales', in the Fulham Road just before the first world war. This picture is taken from the corner of Drayton Gardens looking westward. The two cyclists are telegraph boys.

104. The Queen's Elm pub in the Fulham Road, 1907.

105. The modern Cromwell Road extension spans the vast railway marshalling yards at Earl's Court. The photograph, looking north-west, was taken from the roof of the Empress State Building, offices of the Admiralty.

Knightsbridge

106. Hans Road, Knightsbridge.

107. No small boy today would take his life in his hands by standing in the middle of Beauchamp Place. In Edwardian times the shops were markedly outnumbered by private houses.

108. A theatre poster for Julia Neilsen and Fred Terry in *The Scarlet Pimpernel* at the Vaudeville Theatre dates this photograph of Rutland Gate at 1905.

109. 'Harrods Ltd., Job Masters', reads the sign in Yeomans Row, Knightsbridge. Maid of Honour Row can be seen in the background. All this is now demolished.

110. Patient cabbies wait for fares outside Harrods in Brompton Road. Henry Charles Digby Harrod lived above his shop when he founded it in 1849, and the present terra-cotta building was erected in the 1890s.

111.   Tattersalls at Knightsbridge Green was established in 1864 as a horse auction mart. These gates, with side-entrances and wings, led into nearly two acres of yards and stabling. Demolished in the 1960s and replaced by shops and offices.

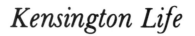

112. In the golden summer of 1914 this little girl proudly led her pony at the annual Donkey, Pony and Baby Show at Tavistock Mews, Notting Hill.

113. This wooden-legged gentleman was the last crossing sweeper in Kensington. A former resident, who gave this photograph to Kensington Public Library, said that she remembered seeing him at the corner of Melbury Road, when as a small child she visited her grandmother at Oakwood Court in 1907.

114. This street musician with his pipes and drum was a familiar sight in Kensington streets in the 1880s.

115 & 116.   These pictures of the Great Wheel at the Earl's Court Exhibition in 1904 give some idea of its vast size. It stood 300 feet high, and was copied from the Ferris Wheel at the Chicago Exhibition. Many people doubted its safety until the Princess of Wales (later Queen Mary) took a ride on it. It did get stuck once, and the passengers, who were marooned all night before being brought down unharmed, were paid £5 each for their trouble.

117. The Imperial Austrian Exhibition at Earl's Court in 1906 took place on exhibition land belonging to the District & Metropolitan railways. There were gardens, an artificial lake with boats and groves of trees. The grounds were used as a refugee camp during the first world war and subsequently lay derelict until the 1930s when the present exhibition complex was built.

118. The International Exhibition held on the site the Natural History Museum in 1862. The nave, seen from the west dome, has an exhibition of Royal Berlin porcelain in the foreground. The designer of this exhibition, Captain Francis Fowke, also designed the Royal Albert Hall.

119. Firemen of Kensington Vestry Fire Brigade pose with
their engine outside the station in Lower Phillimore Mews in
the 1860s.

120. The Headmaster of Kensington Grammar School, the Rev. Mr. Joscelyn, sits with the school secretary among junior boys in the 1880s. The fashions of the day ranged from sailor suits to corduroys and watch-chains.

121. Queen Victoria paid a State Visit to Kensington, the place of her birth, at her Diamond Jubilee on June 28 1897. She is seen here in her landau outside St. Mary Abbots Church, where she was presented with a bouquet by the daughter of the vestry clerk, Beatrice Leete. With the Queen in the carriage is her grandson Prince George, Duke of York (later George V) and his wife Princess 'May' (later Queen Mary).

122. The triumphal archway erected over Kensington High Street, at the eastern end by Kensington Gardens, to celebrate Queen Victoria's Golden Jubilee in 1887.

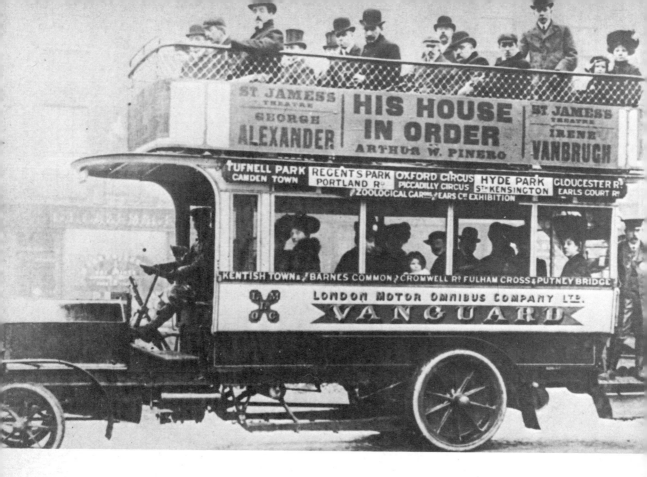

123. A Vanguard bus belonging to the London Motor Omnibus Company on the route between Cromwell Road and Putney in 1906.

124. The Century Motor Mart in Kensington High Street sounds almost modern, but the cars clearly are not. Nor are they cheap, for the £330 asked for the saloon on the left was a large sum of money in 1908, when this photograph was taken.

125 *(overleaf).* Nursemaids by the Long Water in Kensington Gardens.

GARDENS.

126. Originally known as Lord Holland's Lane, Holland Walk was a sunnier place for nursemaids to stop to chat in Edwardian days, before the trees reached their present maturity.

127. Leisurely summer days before the first world war beside the Long Water in Kensington Gardens.

Long Water, Kensington Gardens.

128.   When Barker's delivered by horse and cart!

129. The residents of Market Court in Kensington High Street, demolished in 1869.

130. 'Breakfast and luncheon. 1/- teas only', reads the sign at Kensington Gardens tea-rooms, when the waiters wore straw boaters, and the customers sat in wicker-work chairs.

131. The Hungarian Exhibition at Earl's Court in the 1900s.

132. In 1893, Jubal Webb's mammoth cheese, weighing 22,000 lbs, won highest honours for British produce at the Chicago World Fair. It was later drawn in triumph through the streets of Kensington.

The Western Gardens.

133. Like a solar topee is this elegant bandstand at Earl's Court in 1904.

134. Sailing on the round pond in Edwardian days . . .

136. The famous statue of Peter Pan in Kensington Gardens, soon after its erection.

135. . . . before taking tea in Kensington Gardens.

137. Stalwarts of the 1891 Standard VII at Oxford Gardens School, North Kensington . . .

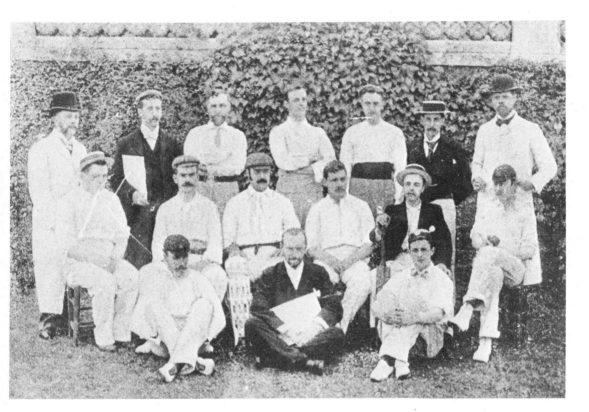

138.　. . . and stalwarts of the Vestry Officials cricket team, who played against the Kensington Vestrymen at Holland Park on June 29 1895.

139. The Brompton Oratory in South Kensington.

140. Nursemaids in Abingdon Villas, off the Earl's Court Road, round about the
time Miss Clementine Hosier lived in one of the houses, from which she married
Winston Churchill in 1908.

141 & 142. Victorian flats in Kensington — Campden Hill Court, still standing, and Thackeray Court in Palace Gate, demolished in the 1970s.

106   LONDON. — *Knightsbridge.* — LL.

143. The entrance from Kensington to central London — Knightsbridge, at the junction of Sloane Street, with a terrace of elegant houses on the left where now the Bowater Building stands.